Away

poems by

Jenna Wysong Filbrun

Finishing Line Press
Georgetown, Kentucky

Away

Copyright © 2023 by Jenna Wysong Filbrun
ISBN 979-8-88838-283-7 First Edition
All rights reserved under International and Pan-American Copyright Conventions. No part of this book may be reproduced in any manner whatsoever without written permission from the publisher, except in the case of brief quotations embodied in critical articles and reviews.

ACKNOWLEDGMENTS

My heartfelt appreciation to these publications in which the following poems from this volume first appeared, often in earlier forms:

"Joy"—*Amethyst Review*

"After Spotting a Barred Owl in the Pine Tree"—*Blue Heron Review* and *T.S. Poetry Every Day Poems*

"Maple on the Hill"—*Crosswinds Poetry Journal*

"Church" (Pushcart Prize Nominee 2021) and "Aspiration"—*The Dewdrop*

"Perspective"—*Red Letter Christians*

"Prayers for Perpetuity in a Place of Change"—*Snapdragon Journal*

"A Good Spot"—*Wild Roof Journal*

Publisher: Leah Huete de Maines
Editor: Christen Kincaid
Cover Art: Jenna Filbrun
Author Photo: Michael Filbrun
Cover Design: Elizabeth Maines McCleavy

Order online: www.finishinglinepress.com
also available on amazon.com

Author inquiries and mail orders:
Finishing Line Press
P. O. Box 1626
Georgetown, Kentucky 40324
U. S. A.

Table of Contents

I.
It Started Here in March 1
In Power's Way 2
Away 3
Maple on the Hill 4
Late October 5
November Trees 6
Little Wren 7
A Prayer for the Day 9
Knowing 10
The Old Existence in Two Movements 11
Solidarity 13
One 14
Exposure 15
Cold 16
Sparrows in the Pine 17
The Doe 18
Adrift 19
Red, Green, Purple 20
The Operating Room 21
Grace 22
Down Into Loss 23

II.
Learning How to Pray 27
Hearing the Leaves Fall 28
For Suffering 29
New Year 2022 30
Perspective 31
Breach 32
Looking 34
Another Omicron Dream 35
Aspiration 37
Lifting 38
Another March, After Much Time 39

III.
Where He Went 43
Inside Grandpa's Barn 44
A Posthumous Appearance 45
Elijah 46
Death of a Sycamore 48
In May Again 49
8:05 a.m., That Morning 50
Like Berry Brambles 51
Hands 52
A Good Spot 53
Dangerous 55

IV.
After Spotting a Barred Owl in the Pine Tree 59
If You Stay Inside, You'll Miss It 60
The Owl Again 61
Prayers for Perpetuity in a Place of Change 62
Joy 63
Turning 65
Snow Melt 66
Silence on the Summit 67
A Real Story 68
Church 69

Biography and Additional Thanks 71

For the millions of lives lost worldwide to COVID-19,[1]
including those in poorer countries without early access to the vaccine,
and many in the United States living in poverty,
disproportionately people of color.
People in the US living in low-income communities
have died from COVID-19
at nearly two times the rate of people in wealthier areas.[2]

---

[1] The World Health Organization's COVID-19 Dashboard lists the count at 6.9 million as of June 2023. Excess mortality data from 2020-2021 suggest 7 million is a vast undercount. For updated numbers and more, see: https://covid19.who.int/ and https://www.who.int/data/stories/global-excess-deaths-associated-with-covid-19-january-2020-december-2021

[2] A study released by The Poor People's Campaign in April 2022 in partnership with the UN Sustainable Solutions Development Network and other organizations, found in an analysis of 3,200 counties in the United States that COVID-19 deaths among people living in poorer counties were nearly two times that of people living in wealthier counties. During the Delta wave, death rates were *five times* higher in these low-income counties. The counties in the poorest tenth percentile contain an overrepresentation of residents of color. https://www.poorpeoplescampaign.org/pandemic-report/

Also in memory of Norma and Don Wysong

"This journey from order to disorder to reorder must happen for all of us…We all come to wisdom at the major price of both our innocence and our control."

—Richard Rohr

I.

It Started Here in March

Unknowns emerge all at once,
like ants flying from the ground.
Normal activity grinds to a stop.
Panic and ignorant defiance

take wing and lodge in the airways
of the most vulnerable.
Another rock on the backs
of the burdened.

But in the woods,
the bare, brown, winter-worn woods,
a cluster of purple crocuses
crowns the crest of the bank.

Out of the decomposed leaves
and snow-swept earth along the canal,
comes this congregation of petaled parishioners
gathered in upside down silk gowns of beaming violet.

A permissible assembly
with a message for the uncertain,
the solitary roamers—
Spring is still on.

In Power's Way

Swarms of blood-sucking realities
rise and buzz
as I swat at them
with my little statements
in my bed.

Calmly,

As I falter along
in the outhouse of nausea,

I do

in the taunting.

what I can.

Away

I listen all day to the wind
in the trees.

It rustles in the sycamores,
shimmers in the cottonwoods,

flutters in the maples,
twirls in the oaks.

Sometimes it is casual;
sometimes in a hurry.

Sometimes it hides
behind the birds and the crickets.

Sometimes it prevails
over all other sounds.

It is deep, full,
constant.

The longer I listen,
the more it becomes—

yes, wind,
but also, somehow,

the sound of all
that is necessary.

Maple on the Hill

for our healthcare workers

A palace of golden light
shines above the roadside.
Bark like the backs
of work-worn hands
drenched in ivy—
deep green.
Bottomless green
on bright gold.
Branches twinkle and shimmer
over the shams of the shallow
winds that can't break it.
Calm truth sifts down
in small pieces—
perfect leaves of five points
and velvet gold.
Each a word of courage
spoken into the madness
of autumn and its slow deaths.

Late October

I close the windows
   to the cold.
      The wind that sat all summer
         in the cottonwood trees
           has risen to carry in
               the crystal masses.

November Trees

The forecasts say it will snow
by the end of the week.
The heavy, white-gray sky
and gusty wind confirm it.

Bare trees rattle in the blasts.
Gone are the stunning hues
their leaves wore at death.
The trees exchange
their rustling scarlets and golds
for this spindly knocking.

Down to their stark selves,
they keep living—
Stand and creak
against months of furious wind.
Then, only when the time
is exactly right,
try again to bloom.

Little Wren

At night, in a dream,
I am in another storm.
A tornadic wind
of bright, hot air
presses me into
the seat of the car
so that I can't move
or breathe.

During the day,
a little wren
lands on the patio step
and squawks
into the frozen air.

At first, I think
the sound of it
is the refrigerator
gone bad, but no.
I follow the noise
to the door to find
this plump, neckless
little ball of feathers,
asking, it really seems,
to be let inside.

The bird twists its head
with each cry,
the barb of its beak
barely cracking open.
The toothpicks of its feet
scrape the sheet of solid ice
on the step as it hurtles
out its protestations.

It flies off, then,
and I hear again
only the whirr
of the furnace
and the occasional
crack of the house
as it shifts in the cold.

A Prayer for the Day the Cottonwood Trees Were Cut Down for Money

God of the wind and its rustling
in the leaves of the old trees,
save us from ourselves, I pray.
Let us not destroy everything good
You have made in Your holiness.
The light in our hearts goes out.
We are left with self-destruction,
hell-bent on total desecration.
Here are the bodies crashing,
the screams of the bones sawn apart.

Knowing

The pasture leans toward
the cottonwood grove
in a gradual dip near the fence corner.

Parts of the felled trees are still there
in the cupped hand of the field.
Piles of parts on the bare ground.

The land holds them up
as an exhibit of how power
tramples the unprotected

to line its own pockets.
Cuts off their feet
and tells them to get going.

Leaves their remains
to rot
in the field.

The Old Existence in Two Movements

1.

Two cats
with a conjoined leg
tumble with a river
toward a gushing waterfall.

They strain and struggle
for shore. Separate efforts
negate progress as each
flails against the other.

An onlooker tries to help,
but the flying claws
and gnashing teeth
gash the outstretched hand.

The rescuer pulls back in surprise.
The current sucks
the sorry pair
into the headwaters.

They travel a smooth slide
with the clear water
into the bottomless
froth and mist below.

2.

Two plants begin to wilt
as they live in a single pot,
crowding for space.

I extract one of them
and transplant it
in a separate container.

Overnight,
they both grow
to the ceiling.

Solidarity

I am early enough
to see the stars
and the silver trees
with their gray shadows.

The long cold raps
on the hardening trunks
to see if they are ready.
Almost.

I'm out with my little dog,
among friends at last.
The stars. The trees.
The black sky. The sharp air.

One

What I need most
is this warm ball
of little dog,
whose soft self
welds my worn-out soul
to the perfect peace
of his silent slumber.
He knows it
and camps at my side.
Sometimes it's the tip of one paw.
Others, a full-body sidle.
But always some conduit
for the current to run
back and forth between us.
I'm ok if you're ok.

Exposure

In a pelting sleet-snow-rain,
a squirrel scrabbles up a fence post
to escape the caking slush.
It squints its black-bead-eyes
against the driving bits of ice.
Wears the coat of its luscious tail.
Sits that way for hours.
Waiting.

Cold

When the sun rises,
the empty trees
are full of light.
They wear
the unbearable cold
of the frost
like diamonds
on their dark bodies
and sway a little
as they sparkle
in the mirrors of themselves
with soft clacks that patter
over the stillness.

Sparrows in the Pine

When sun breaks
into the subzero
morning cold,
we go to the pine
and pick a roost
on the east side.
We puff out
our little red chests.
The tangerine light
makes us glow
like a smatter of rubies
against the blue green needles.
Just when you thought
there was no color left
but the muted tones of winter,
here we are.

The Doe

She is small-boned, a little gangly. A short, well-formed face with the signature round, brown eyes and long, busy ears. She travels alone.

She steps out of the trees most evenings between 5:45 and 6:00. She leaves her comet-like prints through the snow in the pasture and leaps through the hole in the fence to pick her way toward the evergreen shrubs along the drive.

She paws and eats for a few minutes, then continues across the road, down toward the swamp.

We keep this appointment with her, posting ourselves at the window each frozen close of day. Even Oliver is no longer alarmed at her solitary, routine life.

When spring thaws the ground and makes food more abundant, she stops coming.
I am glad for her.
I am.

Adrift

Inch-high waves
lap the canoe's sides—
a steady slap of seconds.

Water in all directions.
Blue, black, silver tessellations
of wind-disrupted silk.

No paddle.
No shore.
No timeline.

At the mercy
of the wind's light wisps
and the water's shifting.

Red, Green, Purple

For nights now, I dream
of a thing coming into being
from the slow blend
of other things that seemed
always before to be
entirely distinct and finished.

Last night, for example,
I dreamed of red and green
pooling and mixing
to become purple.

It isn't a nice dream.
It feels like I am bound,
like the thing should be stopped,
and I can't stop it.
Then, as if time crawls
when it would be best
to have it done with.

Purple is a very nice color.
I'm glad it exists.
I'm glad to remember
how other colors
surrender to become it.
But red
and green?

The Operating Room

                              This time, in a dream, my teeth,
        instead of crumbling
              and spewing out,
                      will be removed.
    I can't understand why.
      I am in the operating room.
            The masks and gowns
                        scurry over their instruments.
      Panic screams in my throat.
                Someone sees me
                      and puts a stop to the preparations.
    He wheels me out of the room
                to a quiet place and says
          he won't let them continue
                      until I'm ready.
I tell him I don't know
if I'll ever be ready.
            The truth in the air between us
                      is a warm pocket of wind
    folded into the cold shards
            of all the other winds.

          He puts a hand on my arm
                      and goes on to the next patient.
    I can't spend the rest of my life here.
I don't want to give them my teeth.

Grace

Like rolling through the frigid,
sick dark into the calm warmth
of your arms in the covers

is the turning
from exasperation
over my weakness

into the grace of my small place
in the chaos and confusion
of nothing and every little thing.

Down Into Loss

I am at the bottom.
I shoveled out all the fury
to find what lay beneath.
I look up and see
the crumbling mounds
for what they are—
a hopeless rescue effort.

Fury won't stop this.

I lean the shovel against the side
and kneel in the cold earth.
I gather grains of it in my hand
and watch them slide out
as dust, like everything.

Snow begins to fall in soft,
perfect symmetry.
A slow drop in the silence.
It buries even the broken earth
in a sparkling cover, one
cold, carefully-crafted crystal
at a time.

II.

Learning How to Pray

Today, I look inside myself and say,
I don't know how to pray anymore.
Then, I look out.

A piney squirrel
skitters over the treetops
as if on solid ground.

A trail of leaves loops
on the wind in its wake,
easily unfastened

in the brittle stages
of turning toward
colorful death.

I write this down.
A clue.

Hearing the Leaves Fall

The silver maples are motionless
as they shed the frost-laden
sheen of their yellow glory
with a rustle like wind
in the steam-rising stillness.

A loss that is, to the trees,
something to flash
into the sideways light,
shuffle into the silence
of the early cold,

share into
the uncertain open,
like singing.

For Suffering

There are days it is not hard
to turn away, to widen out,
and there are days the cold wet presses
into my bones like so many smothered stories.

I take it collectively,
ever since I found myself
in power's way
and started to look around.

If God suffers, if we all suffer,*
I am suddenly a full person
who can exist just like this.
With pain.

Suffering requires lament before joy.
Otherwise, you will dream
over and over you are choking
on a huge pill you can't swallow.

I love the ones like me
and the serious sufferers.
So I listen and learn
from the heavy lifters.

I walk through doorways
into the open where God is,
in all God's glory, everywhere.
In the cloud, and in the light.

---

*Thanks to Richard Rohr for this understanding.

New Year 2022

Again, it is the steam
in the teapot screaming.
The end of nothing, really.
It is time passing.
The lights coming down.
The truth coming out.
It is cruelty on the swell,
the sweep, the overtake.

It is also this house.
The cover of quiet.
It is the watch of the trees.
The wind coming and going.
It is candles still burning,
soft bodies warming.
It is love holding true,
lasting and outlasting.

Perspective

Maybe
I need to climb the hill
of seeing God
nowhere
before I can glimpse
the peaks
of God everywhere.

Am I close?

The light broadens
on the path ahead.
Deep blue between the trees
might soon reveal the curves
and loveliness
of a vast, captivating
beyond.

I travel alone

in courage and fear, trying too hard
and not hard enough. Turning, turning,
I overcompensate and irritate,
push and prod, trudge and plod,
drag and discard, rethink and roam,
forward, blindly, into reality
I hope is just too big to recognize

yet.

Breach

1.

There is a feral cat in the sun by the barn,
pausing for warmth as it passes through.
It has a gash behind one of its ears—
both ears hairless, swollen, red, oozing.

When it leaves, it slink-waddles slowly
through the snow. I pray when it dies,
it will die quickly, despite my disbelief
in the alteration of events by wishful prayer.

The shatter of it
is the shatter of the loves
that turned out to be
convenience in disguise.

I turn away, but the garble of the cat's mew
through half-shut eyes keeps surfacing.
I'm moving the clothes to the dryer,
I'm frying an egg for lunch,

I'm telling the dog everything is ok,
when suddenly, there it is—
this deeper thing needing some air,
hoisting itself into the present.

I tend to it finally,
how suffering has its way.
I feel it down to the deep.
This is my best prayer.

2.

Walking the loop, I pull back
my cramped, winter-wrapped neck
to find the lace of the silver maple branches
budded out on this 13-degree morning.

I huff in surprise, and my breath
drifts up into the buds, then wafts
and swirls around them.
There is no other sign of spring.

No recent warmth, no melting
of the thick, hard snow.
No birds come back to sing,
not yet.

The calm certainty of the trees
despite any external evidence
cracks the veneer of my winter-stiff resolve.
Inside pulses the connection that is my breath

brushing by the red-brown bulbs.
It is the euphoria of the summit,
the old hope for the goodness of people.
The loves that turned out to be real.

This leaping thing launches me
out of the waters of unfeeling
toward love.
I lean into that. A way opens.

Looking

The night after a snow,
I can see clear to the woods
from the window

a grayscale impression
of all the usual things—
the barn, the maple, the fence row.

Not sharp, but vivid.
Essence more visible than edges
in the numinous glow.

I look for the deer
whose prints I find
in the mornings.

I peer into
the east pasture.
They are there.

Three willowy forms
nosing through the snow
under the oak trees.

Contours and curves
dark in the white night,
they bend and beam

the turquoise light.
A kind of music plays,
like a river running.

Another Omicron Dream

I was in a house
made for meditation.
Every corner sparse, pristine.

It was a place for broken people.
Everyone looking for relief,
for each other, for a way through.

"When you hear the alarm,
go to the walls," said the director,
"Sometimes, there is shaking."

When I heard the clang
break the quiet,
I went and clung

to the carpeted wall.
    Some kind of centrifugal force
        pressed me to it as the house

    tumbled and shook.
        This happened at times,
    between the calm of the quiet together.

        We weren't surprised.
    We tried to understand, even as we could not understand,
        even as we were beginning more and more

    not to need to understand.
        We were, in fact, no longer
  afraid of being afraid.

(This is the way it is.)
Even the thrust and rattle
of harm and blame

could not stop us now.
We were living
so much farther into heaven.

Aspiration

The cottonwoods in the back pasture
stretch a hundred feet into the sky
and under the earth,
through eras of people,
to hold the wind
and release things into it—
the snow of their seeds in spring,
sheets of yellow-gray leaves in fall.

They bob and twist their tops
in summer storms
and flutter their tips in the sun.
They freeze fast
to clear winter nights
under the moon,
dewdrop-still.

Lifting

Yesterday, a friend
who really knows about living with pain
reached out of the shadows
with a little light
and told me it is ok to be
right where I am.

Today, I shine that out
the way the ice
under the trees that grow
in the half-frozen swamp
catches the sun
and flashes it back.

Before long, the thin ice
at the base of the tree trunks
pulls up from the swamp water.
It snaps and lifts with the sun,
higher and farther away.
I'm telling you, love

does exist.
I, too, am breaking
toward it.

Another March, After Much Time

First came the muddy flood
of unlove that blasted
from the sky in a matter of hours.
The brown water of death
by cold lies told to paint
self-interest holy and brave
was all over the ground.
It crept up the trees, into the barn,
up into the house.

Then a hard sleet—
the inadequacy of teeth
breaking apart and spewing
out of the mouth, the solid
freeze of fragments held
in cupped hands—
an offering to honesty.

Next a long snow that fell
one flake at a time in torrents
to create the thick, cold cover
that locked all of life
into place.

Now, V's of geese fly honking
over small mounds
of gritty snow in the shadows.
Wetness drips and drains
into the dry ground,
the thirsty rivers.
The wind blows hard.
Soon, the spring peepers
will be croaking.

I'll be coming out, too,
but soggy, toothless, frozen,
wind-burnt, warm, and sprouting.
Much different than
before it all happened.

III.

Where He Went

Death means something new
when someone from your own heart
is on the other side of it
somewhere.

Then it is hard to forget—
no longer a distant inevitability,
but a throat-gripping promise.
Even in springtime.

Like that May we sat in silence
with Grandpa's ashes
in the chirping ground.
I don't know, really,

where he went.
The thick smoke of that
takes up all the space
in my head.

Inside Grandpa's Barn

The old way rides in
on the first whiff
of dust and hay.

Scattered papers, half-cut wood,
cobwebbed saddles, curry combs
in the bucket by the door,

the gnawed edges of the feed troughs
yellowed in the dark corners
all radiate it

the remains
the ghosts
of that heaping life.

A Posthumous Appearance

In a dream, Grandpa
tells Dad to tie a rope around a dead tree
so he can hold the other end from atop the horse
and gallop away to pull it over.

I tell Grandpa
this seems like a bad idea,
even for someone
who already died.

He gives me that twinkle eye
grin that says, with relish,
"We're breaking the rules,
especially because you don't like it."

Then a crack of thunder
whips me awake.

He is gone the way
my eyes see blue for a few seconds
after lightning
bright whites the whole sky,

then see
just the darkness.

Elijah

He eyed me
from high on the piano.
No one I'd ever seen
had a head like that—
an aberrant squash
with drooping eyes
and sagging mouth.

I asked many questions:
"Why is he here?
What happened to the rest of his body?
Why is he so upset?"

"It is made of wood," said Grandma,
"It is not alive and never was."
Still, I carried on
until Elijah went in the closet.

Much later, he made a fresh appearance
on the landing with the other artwork.
Ceramics with night sky glazes,
jars of smooth, white stones,
and that head—
droll and ominous as ever.

"Remember how
you were so afraid of that,"
Grandma chuckles,
"I used to put it away
when you were coming over."

"Yes," I reply, "Look at it."
"Oh pshaw," she laughs,
with a playful shove to my shoulder.
We proceed down the stairs
to pay the bills and sort out the calendar.

These days, the sticky web of dementia
traps and sucks the life out of short-term things.
While Grandma brings the extra chair,
I slip the now-incendiary pieces of mail
into my purse to address alone later.
A familiar gesture of grace.

Death of a Sycamore

We are on the bridge when a fast car appears.
We have to canter the horses to clear it in time.
I'm young and afraid of everything.
I look up at the white sycamore on the other side, close my eyes,

and hang on to the saddle horn as we break into a run.
We cross the bridge in plenty of time, but Grandpa says,
"You need to learn how to canter." Everything in me
prefers a predictable walk. No matter. We pass under the sycamore

into the field where I will learn. Right now.
"You're letting the motion throw you around," Grandpa says,
as I slam into the saddle. "You have to lean in and absorb it in your knees
like this." He coasts and dips with Dice's gate as his hawk-feathered hat floats

along the corn tassels, away and back.
He pulls up in a whirl of dust and pounding hooves
and says, with the twinkle, "Now, try again." I do.
From the sycamore to the end of the field. Until the rhythm snaps into place.

This week the massive sycamore
broke in a strong wind. The road closed
as workers cleared away the debris of its body.

When the crew finished, I went and stood
next to the gray skin of the old stump.

In May Again

Just when the pear trees
soften into white rounds
of pungent petals,
and the grass plumps
to a thicker green,
there will be another death.
Before the peonies open
their magenta puffs this time,
but after tiny bits of green
sprout from red casings
along every branch
and start to uncurl.

8:05 a.m., That Morning

A faint shadow glides
over the ceiling
and draws with it
a cloak that covers me
in the joy of you.

An inside joke.
A favorite old story.

A brief slow down.
Yellow sky, heavy air,
leaf-crinkle-quiet.

Full of laughter.
Can you believe this?
I know. You know.

How Was I So Lucky?

Like Berry Brambles

Now it is time to switch us out,
you for me at the house.
I begin with the contents
of cupboards and drawers.

Pictures, letters,
clippings stashed
for keeps.

Your journal with
my letter of thanks
and reflection.

That reading list
you started to which
I added my notes.

The memorial you wrote
for C. and asked me
to read at the service.

Piles of photos in which you appear.
Young, old, with others, alone—
always smiling.

Even when I close my eyes,
there you are
smiling.

It is painful, delicious work—
To pluck the precious bits
as grief scrapes at the skin.

Hands

I have my grandmother's hands.
When three new age spots
appear below my left index finger—
like a moon and two stars out of the blue
gray sky of early night, I smile.

I remember her hands,
the ridges and veins of ninety-two years,
left pinky crooked outward,
covered in a carpet
of faint brown stars.

She was a potter.
I can see the wet, gray clay
squish through those hands—
held steady against the spinning wheel,
leaving something magnificent.

Like this cup I hold
on this cold morning.
My newly-spotted hands
cradle the smooth
curves her hands formed.

If the night sky develops on my own skin,
I will get to see her fade in
through the years on our hands.
Our long, boney, elegant,
intergalactic hands.

A Good Spot

In this tidy, beribboned bag
are the ashes of one
sixteen-year-old dog.
The owner of the flash
of tongue to face,
the hot chase of piney squirrels
along the fence-top,
a fierce love of vegetables,
keep-away, and soft blankets,
a selective snuggling that,
when given, warmed
like morning coffee going down.

We will bury the ashes
under the sycamore tree
in the back pasture.
As near as possible
to understanding
how a body can become
nothing but dust
and also become
more than it ever was—
something the tree
seems to know.
I can't say how, exactly.
A cellular knowing
gleaned from decades
of not needing to know.
So, we will nest the ashes
under the tree's branches,
where the need to know
comes closest to falling away,
with all other impermanence,
and everything intertwines.
Still, as we plant the ashes
of another love in the ground,

I only feel
the sharp wrench
of now.

Dangerous

I can't seem to love loosely.
To hold my loves at arm's length.
I'm told this is dangerous.

Dangerous, I say, like
scaling a mountain is dangerous.

Dangerous to stand on the edge
of space and time
and peer into the rolling folds
of unknowable things.

To live into the Kingdom Come
I've been asking for my whole life.

IV.

After Spotting a Barred Owl in the Pine Tree

I dream that dream
where I am upstairs
in my great-grandparents' house.

I open a bedroom door to find
the whole annex of timbered rooms
and passageways I never knew existed.

Outside, a flock of barred owls
splits the sky in linear formation
and flies toward me.

They land on the window ledge.
I lift the pane and slide
in among them.

Deep, dark stares gleam at me
from their marbled faces
with complete unsurprise and welcome.

I feel the same as I do in the aspen grove
straddling the tree line,
having shed the layers of things,

or in the bed at the end of the day,
having joined the clump
of our breathing.

I lose track of my edges.

If You Stay Inside, You'll Miss It

The wind blows
hard in the spring.
Great, gasping blasts
drive last year's still-loose-leaves
toward the horizon.
When this gusting wind comes,
you must go out in it.

Deep in it.
Only then will you feel the first
thread of warm sewn into the cold spikes,
hear how the birds sing right through it,
see how the trees respond, and the earth,
budding out.

You will see
how each bud appears at first
as just another knot on a bare branch,
until one day, about the time green
overtakes translucent brown on the ground,
a bit of bright green comes poking through
the now deep red. Then, you, too, might broaden
and be new.

But it takes a long time
to get out of winter.
And don't forget how you will go back in.
How its beauty, too, is deep
if you fall into it.

The Owl Again

Last night, the owl
was in the pine trees.
We heard his voice

in the dark with a start,
a sudden douse of the house
in his questions.

In the morning, we looked
for him in the branches,
hoping to catch him asleep

and get a good eye-full.
If he was there, we didn't see him.
He comes near only sometimes

and not for long. But often
and long enough for me to know
he is not all in my head.

I wouldn't love him the same
if he were tame. If he didn't fly
and land. If he didn't call out

in the dark to give my bones
a shiver. If he wasn't hidden
and only sometimes revealed.

Prayers for Perpetuity in a Place of Change

I writhe on the wet pavement

.

∞

.

Out

.

∞

.

in the rain, I am unearthed,

.

∞

.

Be

.

∞

.

even severed, I survive,

.

∞

.

Yes

.

∞

.

I swallow earth by the mouthful

.

∞

.

Grace

Joy

> *In the upstairs room, the resurrected Christ*
> *is recognized by the wounds*
> *on his new-old body,*
> *still bearing the marks of pain.*
> *(John 20:19-31)*

God, of course, does not protect you
from anything, any more
than anyone else.
And atrocities abound everywhere.

It is spring.
The house down the road
blooms out in its purple
crocus daffodil carpet.

God is a slight heaviness
around your ears
in the quiet.
That is all.

In the early light,
the singing bloom,
is the long dark
and the frozen silence.

Having suffered
the kind of pain
that made you
wish for death,

you are always afraid
of the kind of pain
that made you
wish for death.

Joy knows this
and never pretends
it isn't true.

You look around
at suffering—
An impossible question.
A deep cavern.

You go in because love goes in.
Someone inside is asking for a prayer.
That asking is the most beautiful prayer
you have ever heard.

Well below any low
you have ever been
lies pain like a seed
buried in the ground.

Deep down
where there is no light.
Where few seem to know
it exists.

But joy knows—
thanks to the long,
hard practice
of not pretending.

You go by the house
with the flowers
and marvel.
It is a gift

you can only accept
from deep
in the bare ground
of what also is.

Turning

What you expect
on a day of late winter wind
is hunkering. Eyes shut. Shoulders
round. Neck down. But what you find,
in the low branches of the still bare, but bud-
filled maple, is a robin with her feathers puffed
out in a light glow of sun. The rays warm the underside
of her body, down to the skin under those wispy
thin layers of fluff. You would like to fall
into the fuzz of that silky gray down.

And maybe you could.

You have hunched into the fierce wind a long time,
which you needed to do. But now you are ready
to turn and open your underside to the sun.
As you do, you find you're talking soft,
walking light, thinking the good in us
might grow up vibrant over the ruins
of the old stones. Might become
the roots, trunks, and branches
that will grow up
to become another
someone's
keeper.

Snow Melt

The stream in the high hills
gushes toward the reservoir
with winter's snow melt.

White mounds of water tumble
and roar down the ravine,
into the pines.

Light flickers in and out
of the crashing water and blue-green hills
as sunlight splits the racing clouds.

The stream's clamor climbs all the way
into the snow-crusted peaks
that tower in all directions.

A person is so small in this wild wonder.
Small enough to toss doubts and stipulations
into the mad rush of water,

the free fall brimming with life,
then merge with a permanence beyond
what is merely fathomable.

Silence on the Summit

The wind holds its breath
for several seconds on the summit.
In that brimming quiet, God is
even where God never seems to be.
Like the heft of consistent sickness
or the smog of collective evil.

Here, things are not as separate
as they usually seem.
I carried sickness and evil up,
but I'm only bringing one thing back down—
mystery, which here, it is possible to wear
like a warm, fleece jacket in the chill air.

A Real Story

Tell me something true.
The one about the water
running over the rocks.
How you sat on the bank
until you forgot you were not
another stone gleaming pink in the sun
and listened until you thought
the trickle and rush ran
right through your skin.

Tell it to me when I'm alone,
when I smash my head on the cabinet door
and can't stop crying.

Tell it to me when I'm sweeping the house,
when I'm brushing my teeth
for the 26,287th time.

Tell it to me as I resist the horror
of the things of which we are capable,
when I'm too sick to do anything but listen.

Tell it to me at the cemetery
and at the old church.

You know the one I mean.
How you waded in, laid down,
and became, more than anything,
the glistening stones of your bones
nestled among the rocks.
How you were so In Love
you thought you could die,
and couldn't that be beautiful?

How when you came out,
you knew what you were.

Church

> *"All important ideas must include the trees,
> the mountains, and the rivers."*
> —Mary Oliver

My church is always unlocked
and always full.
It always welcomes
but never demands.
I'm actually not necessary
at all,
but I'm important
because I'm alive.
When I arrive,
the congregation
is already singing.
"Isn't this glorious?"
they intone.
Elk glide over the tundra
at the tree line
like a cloud, or a vapor.
Streams run over rocks
in the meadows
like a violin.
Clouds pillow the peaks
before rain washes out
all unnecessary accruals.
On and on. Always.
"You are this way, too,"
they insist.
Can that be possible?

Biography and Additional Thanks

Jenna Wysong Filbrun writes poetry as a form of prayer and to connect with other writers and readers in the search for meaning and truth. Her poems rely heavily on nature to explore themes of love, suffering, loss, connection, belonging, and healing.

She is also the author of *The Unsaid Words* (Finishing Line Press, 2020), a chapbook of poems from life with chronic illness. Her work has appeared or is forthcoming in publications such as *Amethyst Review, Blue Heron Review, Crosswinds Poetry Journal, Deep Wild, The Dewdrop, EcoTheo Review, Red Letter Christians, Snapdragon Journal,* and *Wild Roof Journal*.

In addition to reading and writing poetry, Filbrun enjoys working with high school students as a math tutor and tennis coach's spouse. More than anything, she loves to spend time with her husband and their two dogs at home and in the wild.

She would like to thank her husband Mike for reading countless drafts and listening faithfully to her endless struggles and questions, for being her best friend and safe place, and for keeping her together.

She would like to thank her parents, Dawn and John Wysong, for their love and support, as well as Oliver and Lewis, her truest companions, who teach her everything there is to know about grace and bring into her life endless love, joy, and barking.

Finally, she wishes to thank Finishing Line Press, Vanessa Able, Cristina Norcross, and Wally Goulet for the opportunities and support that enabled this book to exist, as well as Nancy Bollero Caslick and Ryan Snider for reading and commenting on various parts of various drafts along the way.

To learn more about Filbrun's work, please visit www.jennawysongfilbrun.wixsite.com/poetry.

www.ingramcontent.com/pod-product-compliance
Lightning Source LLC
Chambersburg PA
CBHW031125160426
43192CB00008B/1114